I0462404

Use the box below to sketch an image of what your idea is, even it is a scribble. You never know, this scribble could turn into a masterpiece!!

Ding! My Idea Diary

_____
_____
_____
_____
_____
_____
_____
_____
_____
_____
_____
_____
_____
_____
_____
_____
_____
_____
_____
_____
_____
_____
_____
_____
_____

Use the box below to sketch an image of what your idea is, even it is a scribble. You never know, this scribble could turn into a masterpiece!!

Ding! My Idea Diary

_____
_____
_____
_____
_____
_____
_____
_____
_____
_____
_____
_____
_____
_____
_____
_____
_____
_____
_____
_____
_____
_____
_____
_____

Use the box below to sketch an image of what your idea is, even it is a scribble. You never know, this scribble could turn into a masterpiece!!

Ding! My Idea Diary

_____
_____
_____
_____
_____
_____
_____
_____
_____
_____
_____
_____
_____
_____
_____
_____
_____
_____
_____
_____
_____
_____
_____
_____

Use the box below to sketch an image of what your idea is, even it is a scribble. You never know, this scribble could turn into a masterpiece!!

Ding! My Idea Diary

_____
_____
_____
_____
_____
_____
_____
_____
_____
_____
_____
_____
_____
_____
_____
_____
_____
_____
_____
_____
_____
_____
_____
_____
_____
_____

Use the box below to sketch an image of what your idea is, even it is a scribble. You never know, this scribble could turn into a masterpiece!!

Ding! My Idea Diary

_____
_____
_____
_____
_____
_____
_____
_____
_____
_____
_____
_____
_____
_____
_____
_____
_____
_____
_____
_____
_____
_____

Use the box below to sketch an image of what your idea is, even it is a scribble. You never know, this scribble could turn into a masterpiece!!

Ding! My Idea Diary

_____
_____
_____
_____
_____
_____
_____
_____
_____
_____
_____
_____
_____
_____
_____
_____
_____
_____
_____
_____
_____
_____
_____
_____

Use the box below to sketch an image of what your idea is, even it is a scribble. You never know, this scribble could turn into a masterpiece!!

Ding! My Idea Diary

_____
_____
_____
_____
_____
_____
_____
_____
_____
_____
_____
_____
_____
_____
_____
_____
_____
_____
_____
_____
_____
_____
_____
_____
_____
_____

Use the box below to sketch an image of what your idea is, even it is a scribble. You never know, this scribble could turn into a masterpiece!!

Ding! My Idea Diary

_____
_____
_____
_____
_____
_____
_____
_____
_____
_____
_____
_____
_____
_____
_____
_____
_____
_____
_____
_____
_____
_____
_____
_____
_____
_____
_____

Use the box below to sketch an image of what your idea is, even it is a scribble. You never know, this scribble could turn into a masterpiece!!

Ding! My Idea Diary

_____
_____
_____
_____
_____
_____
_____
_____
_____
_____
_____
_____
_____
_____
_____
_____
_____
_____
_____
_____
_____
_____
_____
_____
_____
_____

Use the box below to sketch an image of what your idea is, even it is a scribble. You never know, this scribble could turn into a masterpiece!!

Ding! My Idea Diary

_____
_____
_____
_____
_____
_____
_____
_____
_____
_____
_____
_____
_____
_____
_____
_____
_____
_____
_____
_____
_____
_____
_____
_____
_____

Use the box below to sketch an image of what your idea is, even it is a scribble. You never know, this scribble could turn into a masterpiece!!

Ding! My Idea Diary

_____
_____
_____
_____
_____
_____
_____
_____
_____
_____
_____
_____
_____
_____
_____
_____
_____
_____
_____
_____
_____
_____
_____
_____

Use the box below to sketch an image of what your idea is, even it is a scribble. You never know, this scribble could turn into a masterpiece!!

Ding! My Idea Diary

_____
_____
_____
_____
_____
_____
_____
_____
_____
_____
_____
_____
_____
_____
_____
_____
_____
_____
_____
_____
_____
_____
_____
_____
_____

Use the box below to sketch an image of what your idea is, even it is a scribble. You never know, this scribble could turn into a masterpiece!!

Ding! My Idea Diary

_____
_____
_____
_____
_____
_____
_____
_____
_____
_____
_____
_____
_____
_____
_____
_____
_____
_____
_____
_____
_____
_____
_____
_____
_____
_____

Use the box below to sketch an image of what your idea is, even it is a scribble. You never know, this scribble could turn into a masterpiece!!

Ding! My Idea Diary

_____
_____
_____
_____
_____
_____
_____
_____
_____
_____
_____
_____
_____
_____
_____
_____
_____
_____
_____
_____
_____
_____
_____
_____

Use the box below to sketch an image of what your idea is, even it is a scribble. You never know, this scribble could turn into a masterpiece!!

Ding! My Idea Diary

_____
_____
_____
_____
_____
_____
_____
_____
_____
_____
_____
_____
_____
_____
_____
_____
_____
_____
_____
_____
_____
_____

Use the box below to sketch an image of what your idea is, even it is a scribble. You never know, this scribble could turn into a masterpiece!!

Ding! My Idea Diary

_____
_____
_____
_____
_____
_____
_____
_____
_____
_____
_____
_____
_____
_____
_____
_____
_____
_____
_____
_____
_____
_____
_____
_____
_____
_____
_____

Use the box below to sketch an image of what your idea is, even it is a scribble. You never know, this scribble could turn into a masterpiece!!

Ding! My Idea Diary

_____

_____

_____

_____

_____

_____

_____

_____

_____

_____

_____

_____

_____

_____

_____

_____

_____

_____

_____

_____

_____

_____

_____

_____

Use the box below to sketch an image of what your idea is, even it is a scribble. You never know, this scribble could turn into a masterpiece!!

Ding! My Idea Diary

_____
_____
_____
_____
_____
_____
_____
_____
_____
_____
_____
_____
_____
_____
_____
_____
_____
_____
_____
_____
_____
_____

Use the box below to sketch an image of what your idea is, even it is a scribble. You never know, this scribble could turn into a masterpiece!!

Ding! My Idea Diary

_____
_____
_____
_____
_____
_____
_____
_____
_____
_____
_____
_____
_____
_____
_____
_____
_____
_____
_____
_____
_____
_____

Use the box below to sketch an image of what your idea is, even it is a scribble. You never know, this scribble could turn into a masterpiece!!

Ding! My Idea Diary

_____
_____
_____
_____
_____
_____
_____
_____
_____
_____
_____
_____
_____
_____
_____
_____
_____
_____
_____
_____
_____
_____
_____
_____

Use the box below to sketch an image of what your idea is, even it is a scribble. You never know, this scribble could turn into a masterpiece!!

Ding! My Idea Diary

_____
_____
_____
_____
_____
_____
_____
_____
_____
_____
_____
_____
_____
_____
_____
_____
_____
_____
_____
_____
_____
_____
_____
_____

Use the box below to sketch an image of what your idea is, even it is a scribble. You never know, this scribble could turn into a masterpiece!!

Ding! My Idea Diary

_____
_____
_____
_____
_____
_____
_____
_____
_____
_____
_____
_____
_____
_____
_____
_____
_____
_____
_____
_____
_____
_____
_____
_____
_____
_____
_____

Use the box below to sketch an image of what your idea is, even it is a scribble. You never know, this scribble could turn into a masterpiece!!

Ding! My Idea Diary

_____
_____
_____
_____
_____
_____
_____
_____
_____
_____
_____
_____
_____
_____
_____
_____
_____
_____
_____
_____
_____
_____
_____
_____

Use the box below to sketch an image of what your idea is, even it is a scribble. You never know, this scribble could turn into a masterpiece!!

Ding! My Idea Diary

_____
_____
_____
_____
_____
_____
_____
_____
_____
_____
_____
_____
_____
_____
_____
_____
_____
_____
_____
_____
_____
_____
_____
_____

Use the box below to sketch an image of what your idea is, even it is a scribble. You never know, this scribble could turn into a masterpiece!!

Ding! My Idea Diary

_____
_____
_____
_____
_____
_____
_____
_____
_____
_____
_____
_____
_____
_____
_____
_____
_____
_____
_____
_____
_____
_____
_____
_____

Use the box below to sketch an image of what your idea is, even it is a scribble. You never know, this scribble could turn into a masterpiece!!

Ding! My Idea Diary

_____
_____
_____
_____
_____
_____
_____
_____
_____
_____
_____
_____
_____
_____
_____
_____
_____
_____
_____
_____
_____
_____
_____
_____
_____

Use the box below to sketch an image of what your idea is, even it is a scribble. You never know, this scribble could turn into a masterpiece!!

Ding! My Idea Diary

Use the box below to sketch an image of what your idea is, even it is a scribble. You never know, this scribble could turn into a masterpiece!!

Ding! My Idea Diary

_____
_____
_____
_____
_____
_____
_____
_____
_____
_____
_____
_____
_____
_____
_____
_____
_____
_____
_____
_____
_____
_____
_____
_____

Use the box below to sketch an image of what your idea is, even it is a scribble. You never know, this scribble could turn into a masterpiece!!

Ding! My Idea Diary

_____
_____
_____
_____
_____
_____
_____
_____
_____
_____
_____
_____
_____
_____
_____
_____
_____
_____
_____
_____
_____
_____

Use the box below to sketch an image of what your idea is, even it is a scribble. You never know, this scribble could turn into a masterpiece!!

Ding! My Idea Diary

_____

_____

_____

_____

_____

_____

_____

_____

_____

_____

_____

_____

_____

_____

_____

_____

_____

_____

_____

_____

_____

_____

_____

_____

_____

_____

_____

Use the box below to sketch an image of what your idea is, even it is a scribble. You never know, this scribble could turn into a masterpiece!!

Ding! My Idea Diary

_____
_____
_____
_____
_____
_____
_____
_____
_____
_____
_____
_____
_____
_____
_____
_____
_____
_____
_____
_____
_____
_____
_____
_____

Use the box below to sketch an image of what your idea is, even it is a scribble. You never know, this scribble could turn into a masterpiece!!

Ding! My Idea Diary

_____
_____
_____
_____
_____
_____
_____
_____
_____
_____
_____
_____
_____
_____
_____
_____
_____
_____
_____
_____
_____
_____
_____
_____

Use the box below to sketch an image of what your idea is, even it is a scribble. You never know, this scribble could turn into a masterpiece!!

Ding! My Idea Diary

_____

_____

_____

_____

_____

_____

_____

_____

_____

_____

_____

_____

_____

_____

_____

_____

_____

_____

_____

_____

_____

_____

_____

Use the box below to sketch an image of what your idea is, even it is a scribble. You never know, this scribble could turn into a masterpiece!!

Ding! My Idea Diary

_____
_____
_____
_____
_____
_____
_____
_____
_____
_____
_____
_____
_____
_____
_____
_____
_____
_____
_____
_____

Use the box below to sketch an image of what your idea is, even it is a scribble. You never know, this scribble could turn into a masterpiece!!

Ding! My Idea Diary

_____
_____
_____
_____
_____
_____
_____
_____
_____
_____
_____
_____
_____
_____
_____
_____
_____
_____
_____
_____
_____
_____

Use the box below to sketch an image of what your idea is, even it is a scribble. You never know, this scribble could turn into a masterpiece!!

Ding! My Idea Diary

_____
_____
_____
_____
_____
_____
_____
_____
_____
_____
_____
_____
_____
_____
_____
_____
_____
_____
_____
_____
_____
_____
_____
_____

Use the box below to sketch an image of what your idea is, even it is a scribble. You never know, this scribble could turn into a masterpiece!!

Ding! My Idea Diary

_____
_____
_____
_____
_____
_____
_____
_____
_____
_____
_____
_____
_____
_____
_____
_____
_____
_____
_____
_____
_____
_____
_____
_____
_____

Use the box below to sketch an image of what your idea is, even it is a scribble. You never know, this scribble could turn into a masterpiece!!

Ding! My Idea Diary

_____
_____
_____
_____
_____
_____
_____
_____
_____
_____
_____
_____
_____
_____
_____
_____
_____
_____
_____
_____
_____
_____
_____
_____

Use the box below to sketch an image of what your idea is, even it is a scribble. You never know, this scribble could turn into a masterpiece!!

Ding! My Idea Diary

_____
_____
_____
_____
_____
_____
_____
_____
_____
_____
_____
_____
_____
_____
_____
_____
_____
_____
_____
_____
_____
_____
_____

Use the box below to sketch an image of what your idea is, even it is a scribble. You never know, this scribble could turn into a masterpiece!!

Ding! My Idea Diary

_____
_____
_____
_____
_____
_____
_____
_____
_____
_____
_____
_____
_____
_____
_____
_____
_____
_____
_____
_____
_____
_____
_____
_____
_____

Use the box below to sketch an image of what your idea is, even it is a scribble. You never know, this scribble could turn into a masterpiece!!

Ding! My Idea Diary

_____
_____
_____
_____
_____
_____
_____
_____
_____
_____
_____
_____
_____
_____
_____
_____
_____
_____
_____
_____
_____
_____
_____

Use the box below to sketch an image of what your idea is, even it is a scribble. You never know, this scribble could turn into a masterpiece!!

Ding! My Idea Diary

_____
_____
_____
_____
_____
_____
_____
_____
_____
_____
_____
_____
_____
_____
_____
_____
_____
_____
_____
_____
_____
_____
_____
_____

Use the box below to sketch an image of what your idea is, even it is a scribble. You never know, this scribble could turn into a masterpiece!!

Ding! My Idea Diary

_____
_____
_____
_____
_____
_____
_____
_____
_____
_____
_____
_____
_____
_____
_____
_____
_____
_____
_____
_____
_____
_____

Use the box below to sketch an image of what your idea is, even it is a scribble. You never know, this scribble could turn into a masterpiece!!

Ding! My Idea Diary

_____
_____
_____
_____
_____
_____
_____
_____
_____
_____
_____
_____
_____
_____
_____
_____
_____
_____
_____
_____
_____
_____
_____
_____

Use the box below to sketch an image of what your idea is, even it is a scribble. You never know, this scribble could turn into a masterpiece!!

Ding! My Idea Diary

_____
_____
_____
_____
_____
_____
_____
_____
_____
_____
_____
_____
_____
_____
_____
_____
_____
_____
_____
_____
_____
_____

Use the box below to sketch an image of what your idea is, even it is a scribble. You never know, this scribble could turn into a masterpiece!!

Ding! My Idea Diary

Use the box below to sketch an image of what your idea is, even it is a scribble. You never know, this scribble could turn into a masterpiece!!

Ding! My Idea Diary

_____
_____
_____
_____
_____
_____
_____
_____
_____
_____
_____
_____
_____
_____
_____
_____
_____
_____
_____
_____
_____
_____

Use the box below to sketch an image of what your idea is, even it is a scribble. You never know, this scribble could turn into a masterpiece!!

Ding! My Idea Diary

_____
_____
_____
_____
_____
_____
_____
_____
_____
_____
_____
_____
_____
_____
_____
_____
_____
_____
_____
_____
_____
_____
_____

Use the box below to sketch an image of what your idea is, even it is a scribble. You never know, this scribble could turn into a masterpiece!!

Ding! My Idea Diary

_____
_____
_____
_____
_____
_____
_____
_____
_____
_____
_____
_____
_____
_____
_____
_____
_____
_____
_____
_____
_____
_____
_____
_____

Use the box below to sketch an image of what your idea is, even it is a scribble. You never know, this scribble could turn into a masterpiece!!